Need for Speed

Dragsters

by Bizzy Harris

Bullfrog Books

Ideas for Parents and Teachers

Bullfrog Books let children practice reading informational text at the earliest reading levels. Repetition, familiar words, and photo labels support early readers.

Before Reading
- Discuss the cover photo. What does it tell them?
- Look at the picture glossary together. Read and discuss the words.

Read the Book
- "Walk" through the book and look at the photos. Let the child ask questions. Point out the photo labels.
- Read the book to the child, or have him or her read independently.

After Reading
- Prompt the child to think more. Ask: Dragsters are long and thin. How do you think this shape helps them go fast?

Bullfrog Books are published by Jump!
5357 Penn Avenue South
Minneapolis, MN 55419
www.jumplibrary.com

Library of Congress Cataloging-in-Publication Data

Names: Names: Harris, Bizzy, author.
Title: Dragsters / by Bizzy Harris.
Description: Minneapolis, MN: Jump!, Inc., [2023]
Series: Need for speed | Includes index.
Audience: Ages 5–8
Identifiers: LCCN 2021043607 (print)
LCCN 2021043608 (ebook)
ISBN 9781636906720 (hardcover)
ISBN 9781636906737 (paperback)
ISBN 9781636906744 (ebook)
Subjects: LCSH: Dragsters—Juvenile literature.
Drag racing—Juvenile literature.
Classification: LCC TL236.2 .H36 2023 (print)
LCC TL236.2 (ebook) | DDC 629.228—dc23
LC record available at
https://lccn.loc.gov/2021043607
LC ebook record available at
https://lccn.loc.gov/2021043608

Editor: Eliza Leahy
Designer: Emma Bersie

Photo Credits: Raytags/Dreamstime, cover, 1, 4, 5; Al Mueller/Shutterstock, 3; Phillip Rubino/Shutterstock, 6–7, 10–11, 13, 22, 23bl; Matt Woods/Alamy, 8–9, 23br; ZUMA/Alamy, 12, 20–21; John Leyba/Getty, 14–15, 23tl; Yevgen Rychko/Dreamstime, 16; Allan Clegg/Dreamstime, 17; Leo Mason/Popperfoto/Getty, 18–19, 23tr; Andrew Norris/Dreamstime, 24.

Printed in the United States of America at Corporate Graphics in North Mankato, Minnesota.

Table of Contents

Low and Fast 4

Parts of a Dragster 22

Picture Glossary 23

Index 24

To Learn More 24

Low and Fast

What race car is long and thin?

It is a dragster!

It sits low to the ground.

tire

The back tires are big.

The front tires are small.

Wings keep the car stable.

wing

wing

funny
car

A funny car is a kind of dragster.

It is short and wide.

The driver wears a helmet.

helmet

The car has a roll cage.

It protects the driver in a crash.

roll cage

Two cars line up.
They will race
on a drag strip.

14

drag
strip

Lights turn green.

light

The cars take off!

The race is fast.

It only lasts four seconds.

A parachute helps
each car stop.

parachute

19

This race has four cars.
Would you like to
see a drag race?

Parts of a Dragster

A dragster's top speed is 335 miles (539 kilometers) per hour. Take a look at its parts!

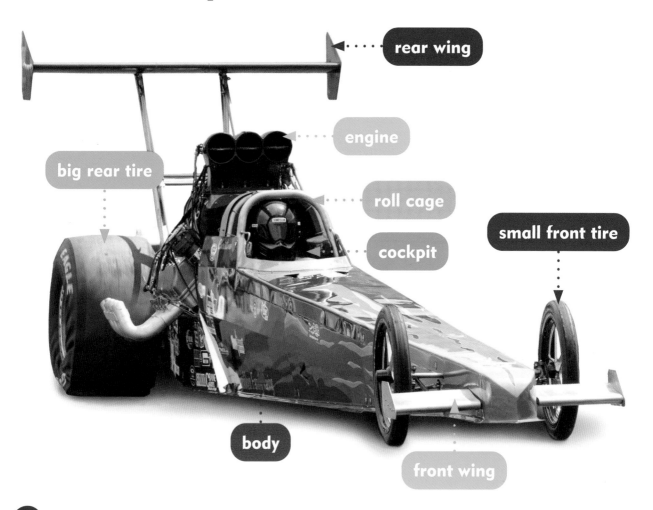

rear wing

engine

big rear tire

roll cage

cockpit

small front tire

body

front wing

Picture Glossary

drag strip
A strip of pavement on which dragsters race.

parachute
A piece of fabric that is attached to ropes and spreads out to slow whatever is attached to it.

protects
Guards or keeps someone safe from harm or injury.

stable
Steady and not easily moved.

Index

crash 13

drag strip 14

driver 12, 13

funny car 11

helmet 12

lights 16

parachute 18

race 14, 18, 21

roll cage 13

stop 18

tires 7

wings 8

To Learn More

Finding more information is as easy as 1, 2, 3.

❶ Go to www.factsurfer.com

❷ Enter "dragsters" into the search box.

❸ Choose your book to see a list of websites.